LOYALTY

LOYALTY
ALL FEATHERS, NO COTTON

CHRIS WILKINS

GIL WILLIAMS

EPISODE 101

"The strength of a family, like the strength of an army, is in its loyalty to each other." - Anon

EXT. STREET - MIAMI GARDENS, FL - EVENING

A sticky, south Florida sun sets on an otherwise uneventful evening in this working class ward 10 miles removed from the glitz and beauty of South Beach.

In the middle of the block sits a well maintained, single story family home. Manicured front lawn. Late model SUV parked under a car port in the driveway.

INT. HOUSE - EVENING

Inside, an attractive woman, RACHEL JOHNSON (Af-Am, 40s), sits at her dining room table writing a card. In front of her on the table is an unfolded letter next to a stuffed animal.

The home is tastefully furnished. Walls filled with art work, family pictures & religious iconography. As she writes, we settle on a PICTURE of her and a cute little boy.

RACHEL (V.O.)

Dear Andre,

From the first time I held you, I knew you were going to be special. I realize this past year hasn't been easy for you, but through it all you've managed to grow into a strong, beautiful young man.

Enjoy your 24th year, take advantage of all that life has to offer, work hard, dream big, and remember to make good choices. They will define your life. You can start with cleaning your room & coming back to church. :) Love, Mom

As she goes to put the card in its envelope, a SILENCED GUN is raised to her head. A MASKED GUNMAN in all black whispers his final goodbye.

MASKED GUNMAN

I'm sorry.

Then PULLS THE TRIGGER. Rachel's lifeless body slumps forward. A dark stream of crimson starts to serpentine across the table, quickly covering the letter, card, and teddy bear.

INT. APARTMENT - EVENING - SAME TIME

ANDRE (24, aka DRE or BOOKS) sits on a bed in a modest studio apartment getting dressed. Though it's been a few years since his high school football days, he's still game fit.

A cute Middle Eastern girl, NAZ (20s), lies on the bed next to him holding a vape pen in post coital bliss. Takes a huge hit.

NAZ

Damn Dre, didn't your mom ever teach you it was rude to hit and run?

She exhales, slightly annoyed. Then reaches for her phone.

NAZ (CONT'D)

At least let me Snapchat that fine ass body. Make all my girls jealous.

DRE

Sorry babe, gotta bounce.

Grabs his keys & phone off the table. Pulls up his pants. Gives her a quick kiss.

DRE (CONT'D) Snap time's over.

EXT. APARTMENT - STREET - MOMENTS LATER

Dre exits the building. As he walks down the street, his phone keeps pinging with happy birthday texts & social media posts.

He crosses the street. Pulls out his phone. Unlocks the door of his 1989 LTD Crown Victoria. Recently rebuilt Ford 302 fuel injected V8. Black with cherry red piping. Sitting on matte black 22s.

INT. HOUSE - DINING ROOM - EVENING

Rachel's body remains splayed out on top of the table. The killer stands with his back to her. Looking at pictures on the wall. One in particular seems to capture his attention:

CLOSE UP: A nighttime picture of Rachel, Dre and his friends laughing and smiling in front of a pink Escalade.

Rachel's phone starts VIBRATING on the table, disrupting the killer's intent gaze. He turns, looks. Sees ANDRE (SON) on the phone screen. A look of recognition flashes in his dark eyes.

INT. CROWN VICTORIA - STREET - EVENING - MOMENTS LATER

Dre hangs up without leaving a message. Drives down a few more blocks. Pulls up to the house, noticing his mom's SUV in the driveway. Quickly parks out front, jerking the Crown Vic to a stop.

EXT. HOUSE - EVENING - MOMENTS LATER

Gets out of the car. Closes his door as he dials out to his mother again. Walks up to the front of the house. Pulls out his keys. Unlocks the door.

INT. HOUSE - EVENING - MOMENTS LATER

Opens it. Goes inside. Notices all the lights are off.

DRE

Ma? I know you're here and you know I don't like surprise parties.

No response. He reaches for the light. Turns it on. TWO more SILENCED SHOTS ring out.

INT. SHILOH BAPTIST CHURCH - MIAMI GARDENS, FL - LATE MORNING

A soulful rendition of "His Eye is on the Sparrow" is sung by the church CHOIR as MOURNERS file past Rachel's casket.

Dre sits in the front pew with his left arm in a sling, wearing a dark grey suit & glasses. His countenance a mask of stone as people file past him offering their condolences.

Next to him are his friends from the picture: DRINO (Cuban/Af-Am, late 20s), ZOEBOY (Haitian, mid 20s), & LALO (Puerto Rican/Cuban, early 20s). All in black suits, devoid of emotion like their deeply aggrieved friend.

As the choir finishes, the FUNERAL DIRECTOR (50s, Af-Am) brings the mourning procession to an end. REV. JAMES ARTHUR WALKER (Af-Am, 40s) steps into the pulpit.

REV. WALKER

I sing because I'm happy, I sing because I'm free. My eye is on the sparrow, and I know he watches me. Can I get an "Amen"?

A chorus of "Amens" ring throughout the sanctuary. The church is completely packed.

REV. WALKER (CONT'D)

Amen. God watches over every one of us with love in His heart. And in His infinite wisdom & tender mercy, grants to all the years of our lives. To some, He grants long, healthy life. Praise the Lord. To others, like our beloved sister Rachel Johnson, whose life we celebrate today, He gifts what seems like only a brief moment.

He pauses, fraught with emotion. A panoply of loud lamentations are heard throughout the room.

REV. WALKER (CONT'D)

But what's important is not the length of our years but the fruit & the service of our years. (MORE)

REV. WALKER (CONT'D)

These are what give meaning to our lives and in her 48 years, Rachel Johnson, honored & glorified the Lord. Amen?

Another round of "Amens" echo throughout the church.

REV. WALKER (CONT'D)

She honored and glorified God with the many students she taught and counseled over the years at Miami Carol City High and in our own Shiloh Sunday school.

Many of her current & past STUDENTS in the congregation wipe away tears.

REV. WALKER (CONT'D)

She honored and glorified the Lord with her many hours working in the Shiloh Soup Kitchen and being a dutiful, devoted mother to her beloved son, Andre.

He locks eyes with Dre, whose silent tears fall beneath the dark glasses.

REV. WALKER (CONT'D)

Now we don't know why God has called our sister home. Why, after defeating the Goliath of breast cancer last year, she was struck down by the dark scourge of violence.

He cuts a look at Drino and the rest of Dre's boys.

REV. WALKER (CONT'D)

And it would be easy to desire retribution. It's very human to want to seek out the killer and exact street justice. Perhaps at a different time in my life, I would've advocated for that.

He pauses, beholding the entire congregation. A mix of tears & unresolved anger fill the sacred space.

REV. WALKER (CONT'D)

But like Romans 12:19 instructs us, "Do not avenge yourselves, beloved, but leave room for

God's wrath. For it is written: "Vengeance is

Mine, I will repay, says the Lord."

EXT. SHILOH BAPTIST CHURCH - DAY - LITTLE LATER

The last few people file out of the sanctuary, offering their final condolences to Dre. His boys remain in solidarity beside him. The funeral director walks up.

FUNERAL DIRECTOR

Andre, it's time to move the body outside. Do you have your pallbearers?

Dre's friend Drino, standing next to him, answers.

DRINO

Right here boss. And these two.

He motions to ZoeBoy and Lalo. The director does a quick count.

FUNERAL DIRECTOR

With Andre that's only four. Normally there are at least 6.

ZoeBoy smiles, flashing his impossibly white teeth. Speaks with a Haitian Creole accent.

ZOEBOY

Don't worry yourself director. We might look like four...

Lalo, the smallest & least buff of the crew, walks over. Puts his arm on the director's shoulder to convey his assurance.

LALO

... but we can move weight like eight.

EXT. SHILOH BAPTIST CHURCH - DAY - MOMENTS LATER

Dre and his friends walk the closed casket out of the church and into the black Cadillac HEARSE parked out front.

A late model MERCEDES S CLASS pulls up across the street. Parks. A handsome, well dressed man, ANDRE SR. (40s) gets out.

Drino, ZoeBoy & Lalo get into the hearse. Dre waits outside. The man crosses the street. Walks up to Dre.

ANDRE SR.

Hey son, sorry I'm late. Had some fires to put out at the office before I could leave. Apparently signing everyone's checks isn't enough. Did you get the flowers?

DRE

Yeah, I got them. The spray of white orchids. You know she was allergic to orchids, right? That pretty much sums up your entire relationship.

The funeral director closes the rear door of the hearse. Turns to Andre Sr.

FUNERAL DIRECTOR

Make sure you turn on your lights if you're following in the procession.

He walks around to the driver's side front and gets in. Starts the engine. Father looks to son.

ANDRE SR.

Alright then, I guess I'll see you over at the cemetery.

DRE

Don't bother. You made your priorities abundantly clear when she was alive. So don't try to pretend now that she's dead.

INT. HEARSE - STREET - DAY

Dre gets in. The hearse pulls off. Like in a limousine, the rear seats face each other. Dre & Lalo on one side. Drino & ZoeBoy across from them. They ride for a while in silence. Dre's glasses are back on. He looks out the window.

DRE

You know this is your fault, right?

Turns his glare to Drino.

DRE (CONT'D)

If you weren't so fucking greedy she might still be alive.

DRINO

I know this is hard on you B, but that's your feelings talking. Look at everything I did... no, everything we did. That was all love. I love your mom, man. We all do. That's famil..

Before Drino can get it out, Dre launches out of his seat, throwing a violent RIGHT HOOK that lands squarely on Drino's jaw. Despite his recovering wounds, the pent up rage inside inures him to the pain.

Lalo & ZoeBoy quickly move to break it up. Eventually manage to separate the two. Drino sits back, as close to vulnerable as he'll ever get.

DRINO (CONT'D)

I am so sorry shit went down like this Books but I promise you, it will not end here. We will burn this bitch down. And fuck what that pastor said. Revenge isn't God's, it's ours.

Dre tries to compose himself, barely clinging to reality. The glazed over look in his eyes of someone who has lost everything.

DRINO (CONT'D)

And a black, deadly, cold ass winter is coming to Miami.

Dre slowly nods in acceptance. As they ride to the cemetery in silence, contemplating their next moves, we RISE UP off the hearse, into the sky and...

<u>LOYALTY</u>

EXT. STREET - MIAMI GARDENS - LATE AFTERNOON

ONE YEAR EARLIER...

We open with a bird's eye view of a YELLOW CAB driving through a mostly industrial neighborhood.

INT. YELLOW CAB - STREET - LATE AFTERNOON

Inside, Drino drives while Dre rides along smoking a blunt & listening to Miami rapper L¥nk$. Drino wears a white wife beater, black jeans & Jordans. Dre's in a mix of grey & black athleisure and Superstars.

DRE

Yo, your boy L¥nk$ is killing it.

He holds the blunt in one hand & a GOLD EMBOSSED double CD case in the other. Built into its side is a polished silver HUMIDOR emblazoned with the name L¥NK$.

DRE (CONT'D)

These invitations are fire and his private label Kush is a straight banger.

DRINO

No doubt B. My head is just about right for this piece.

He parks. Dre takes one more puff then passes it to Drino.

DRINO (CONT'D)

I don't know if this new album's gonna be popping...

Takes the last few pulls. Dots it. Parks the cab.

DRINO (CONT'D)

... but the little muthafucka definitely knows how to throw a party.

EXT. STREET - MOMENTS LATER

They get out. Walk up the street to a warehouse. A 10 ft. SPIKED STEEL GATE stands in front them. Security CAMERA mounted on top. Dre types a code from the CD case into a keypad.

EXT. WAREHOUSE - MOMENTS LATER

The steel gate SLIDES OPEN. Dre & Drino step inside where several luxury vehicles are parked. Walk up to the building.

An infrared sensor is mounted on the wall next to a 14 ft. corrugated steel ROLLING SHEET DOOR. Dre passes the invitation in front of the sensor. The door begins to rise.

INT. WAREHOUSE - FRONT SECTION - MOMENTS LATER

HIP HOP MUSIC plays as Dre & Drino make their way inside. Once in, they are immediately greeted by a hulking BODY-GUARD (30s, face tat). L¥nk$'s tall, model pretty Asian assistant (20s) greets them with two flutes of champagne.

ASSISTANT

Good afternoon gentlemen and welcome.

She hands a glass to each then starts walking. They follow. So does the bodyguard.

ASSISTANT (CONT'D)

If you would be so kind as to deposit any firearms in these safety deposit boxes, it would be most appreciated.

She stops at a wall of secured steel boxes. Dre & Drino share a look.

ASSISTANT (CONT'D)

I can assure you, anything left will be safely secured & returned once the party has concluded. Our superhero sized friend here guarantees it.

The guard nods. Dre pulls out his Beretta. Puts it in one of the boxes. Takes the key.

ASSISTANT (CONT'D)

Thank you. It makes for a much more placid environment.

She places her thumb on a digital scanner.

ASSISTANT (CONT'D)

And besides, why bring a Happy Meal...

A heavy steel door slides open.

ASSISTANT (CONT'D)

... to a nine course gourmet feast?

INT. WAREHOUSE - BACK ROOM - MOMENTS LATER

They step inside. Exhibited all around the room are high end WEAPONS DISPLAYS. Various BUYERS walk around drinking Ace of Spades champagne & checking out the wares.

Rapper L¥NK$ (short, dreads, 30s) walks over. Sports a red Puma sweatsuit, sneakers & thick gold chain. Holds two VIRTUAL REALITY headsets.

LYNK$ Drino, Books glad you brothers could make it.

Hands them each a headset.

LYNK$ (CONT'D)

Before the auction begins, why don't you take a quick tour to better acquaint yourselves with the new album. As you'll see, I've got songs for all occasions.

Dre & Drino don the headsets.

LYNK$ (CONT'D)

The prices listed are the starting bids for each single. Auction goes live in five minutes.

As they begin their virtual tour, the bodyguard comes in holding a sign announcing Miami PD is on the way in.

LYNK$ (CONT'D)

Check that, time for the B-side. He takes their headsets.

LYNK$ (CONT'D)

The bacon boys are knocking at the back door.

As the news quickly circulates throughout the room, guests start scrambling for the exits. Drino heads back towards the front room. Dre follows.

INT. WAREHOUSE - FRONT ROOM - MOMENTS LATER

The steel door slides open. As Drino heads for the boxes, MIAMI PD BARRELS THROUGH the rolling SHEET DOOR in an all black, bullet proof BATTERING RAM SUV.

Dre & Drino jet for the rear EMERGENCY EXIT. The SUV comes to a stop. Two Miami PD OFFICERS jump out. Give chase.

EXT. WAREHOUSE - LOADING DOCK - MOMENTS LATER

Dre & Drino burst through the emergency door, tripping an ALARM.

Jet out onto the loading dock. JUMP DOWN to the lower level.

Start heading for the BARBED WIRE FENCE surrounding the rear of the property. The cops slam through the door after them. Guns drawn.

OFFICERS

Stop now! Miami PD!

Dre & Drino keep going. Race towards a DUMPSTER. Dre hurdles on top. BOX JUMPS over the top of the wire. CLEARS it. LANDS safely on the other side of the fence, his athleticism on full display.

Drino follows suit. Attempts the BOX JUMP but comes up a little SHORT. CLIPS his right foot on the wire, SHREDDING the top of his Jordans & sending him SOMERSAULTING over top.

EXT. STREET - MOMENTS LATER

He CRASHES onto the sidewalk below. Dre helps him up. They start running. Make their way back to the taxi.

Drino limps to the passenger's side. Foot bleeding. Unlocks the doors. Throws the keys to Dre. They jump in. Dre fires up the engine. Peals out of the parking space. Races down the street.

A Miami PD BLACK & WHITE parked in front of the warehouse hits its sirens. TAKES OFF.

Dre whips around a corner, blowing through a STOP LIGHT. T BONES the back of a pick up TRUCK, sending it spiraling out of control and spilling crates of ORANGES all over the street.

INT. SQUAD CAR - STREETS - LATE AFTERNOON

The black & white SMASHES through the strewn citrus. Driving the police car is MILAGROS ESPERANZA (30s, aka M), joined by Miami PD veteran, PETE MCCLUSKEY (40s, Irish, old school). Esperanza grabs her radio.

ESPERANZA

In pursuit of 2 African American males, approximately 20-30, in a yellow taxi headed south on Le Jeune. Suspected of possible gun trafficking.

We'll have a high octane CHASE down SW 42nd Ave/South Le Jeune

Road ending up near NW 21st Street and the exit for Miami International. By this time, several other SQUAD CARS have joined the pursuit.

Despite Miami PD's best efforts, Dre is able to navigate his way into airport traffic, eventually losing the phalanx of black & whites in the sea of taxis, Lyfts & Ubers.

INT. YELLOW CAB - MIAMI INTERNATIONAL AIRPORT - LITTLE LATER

Dre drives around to the Departing Flights level of the Central Terminal. Pulls up to the curb. Parks. Takes off his Superstars. Hands them to Drino.

DRE

Call a Lyft and meet me upstairs at the J Gate pick up area.

Drino nods. Takes off his Jordans. Still in obvious pain. Puts on the Superstars. Gets out. Closes the door. Dre drives back into traffic.

As he makes his way over to the South Terminal, a Miami Airport POLICE CAR pulls in behind him. Follows him for a while but keeps going when Dre pulls into the H Gate taxi stand.

INT. YELLOW CAB - MIAMI INTERNATIONAL - LATE AFTERNOON

Parks. Cuts the engine. Grabs a black BACKPACK from the back seat.

Takes out a pair of rubber GLOVES, roll of PAPER TOWELS & CLEANING SOLUTION. Scrubs the taxi thoroughly. Throws the supplies back into the pack along with Drino's Jordans. Hops out.

EXT. MIAMI INTERNATIONAL AIRPORT - LATE AFTERNOON

Walks over to the next gate. Meets Drino at the designated area just as their Lyft pulls up. Late model Camry. They get in.

INT. LYFT - MIAMI INTERNATIONAL AIRPORT - DUSK

The Camry merges into departing airport traffic. Dre checks behind them. No sign of Esperanza & McCluskey.

DRE

I gave ole girl a bath and scooped your Js.

He opens the backpack. Hands Drino his shoes.

DRINO

Good looks, Books.

Takes off the Superstars. Winces in pain. Dre checks out his foot.

DRE

You should probably get Spells to check that out for you bro. Don't want that shit to get infected.

The Lyft exits the airport. Starts heading south.

DRE (CONT'D)

That's how the dread man Bob Marley died.

EXT. VAN - BACK ALLEY - NIGHT

Lalo drives a beat up industrial VAN down a dark alley. Comes to a stop behind a blacked out Chevy Tahoe. Shuts his lights. Cuts the engine.

EXT. BACK ALLEY - NIGHT - MOMENTS LATER

Out of the Tahoe steps DROP (30s, Dominican, skinny). Lalo hops out of the van. They exchange quick pleasantries.

LALO

Yo, what's goodie my boy?

DROP

Oh, you know, just trying to do this thing.

(motions to the van)

You riding like we talked about?

LALO

Ten 65" curved 4K ultra high def smart screens, all with Kodi. 16 bands.

DROP

Let's say 15 and you help me move them this time. I was blowing this bitch's back out last night and wound up tweaking my own shit.

Lalo considers. After a few beats, he nods in approval. As he leads Drop to the back of the van, another blacked out Tahoe turns the corner.

DROP (CONT'D)

Or, better yet... how about on the house?

The Tahoe drives up. Doors open. Four jail strong THUGS step out.

DROP (CONT'D) In exchange for your life.

Two of Drop's crew flash steel. Lalo decides to play along.

LALO

Eres un pinche puto, sabes? (You're a little bitch, you know that?)

He opens the van's doors. Drop's squad steps up. Start unloading.

LALO (CONT'D)

But that's okay go ahead, karma's a bitch. If you really needed a come up, you should've asked for more product.

They empty the van quickly.

LALO (CONT'D)

But I guess the only things bright around here are the tvs.

INT. NORTH SHORE MEDICAL CENTER - ROOM - NIGHT

A pretty brown skinned girl, FABIOLA (20s, Haitian), lies asleep in a hospital bed. A vital signs MONITORING UNIT rests nearby. ZoeBoy sits at her side. His phone rings. He quickly grabs it. Steps out of the room.

ZOEBOY Como ye.

INT. VAN - STREETS - NIGHT - SAME TIME

Lalo navigates the van down a busy street. Left eye swollen. Busted lip. Has the phone on speaker.

LALO

Yo ZoeBoy, it's Lalo. I just got hit for 16 checks and my merch.

INT. NORTH SHORE MEDICAL - HALL - NIGHT

ZoeBoy stands outside the room. Switches to his Haitian accented English.

ZOEBOY

What? What happened?

LALO (O.S.)

You know that kid Drop?

ZOEBOY Little Dominican from west HIA?

LALO (O.S.)

Yeah, him. We met up like always. Little muthafucka came four deep this time. Everybody swoll like they just did a dime at the state B&B.

ZOEBOY So why you telling me?

LALO (O.S.)

I heard the Road Runnas might be looking to expand.

A young, harried NURSE (30s, brunette) walks up to ZoeBoy.

NURSE

I'm sorry sir but visiting hours are about to be over.

He covers the phone. Nods his head.

LALO (O.S.)

You think you could arrange a sit down with Drino & Dre for me?

ZoeBoy goes back in the room. Kisses Fabiola on the forehead.

ZOEBOY

I'm about to see them both at Dre's birthday party.

Grabs his jacket. Starts heading out.

ZOEBOY (CONT'D)

Let me see what I can do.

INT. HOUSE - BATHROOM - MIAMI GARDENS - NIGHT

Dre and Naz engage in a heavy makeout session in Rachel's bathroom. She raps on the door.

RACHEL

Andre Julius Johnson, I know you are not disrespecting my bathroom!

After a few seconds, the door quickly swings open. Dre walks out first. Casts his eyes downward.

RACHEL (CONT'D)

It might be your 24th birthday but you are not that grown.

Naz follows, in her own walk of shame. Tries to quickly fix herself up.

RACHEL (CONT'D) Hold it.

Naz freezes. Rachel adjusts her collar. Winks in tacit approval. Sends her off back to the party.

INT. HOUSE - LIVING ROOM - MOMENTS LATER

The house is full of family and friends, many of whom we'll recognize from the funeral. A mix of hip hop and R&B music plays. A good time is being had by all.

Dre works his way through the crowd. Standing near the front door holding a bottle of Crown Royal Apple is ZoeBoy.

ZOEBOY

Bon anni mon frère.

Hands Dre the bottle. They start making their way through the party.

ZOEBOY (CONT'D)

How'd everything go with L¥nk$?

Dre cracks the bottle open. Takes a few big hits.

DRE Ran into a slight delay but we'll work it out.

He stashes the bottle in a closet. Closes the door.

ZOEBOY

Hey, you remember my boy Lalo?

DRE

The Spanish kid who does the credit thing? What about him?

ZOEBOY

He wants to meet with us. Got pinched for his merch and I think he's looking for back up.

DRE

What are we mercenaries? You know this dude like that?

ZOEBOY

Not really but I know he's got heart. Helped me out of a tight spot right after I moved here.

DRE

Alright, I'll call Drino. Check and see if my mom needs any help in the kitchen.

INT. HOUSE - KITCHEN - MOMENTS LATER

Rachel stands at her kitchen island frosting Dre's birthday cake. A tray of hot wings and bowl of guac sit nearby, next to a plastic bowl and unopened bag of tortilla chips. ZoeBoy walks in. Gives Rachel a kiss on the cheek.

ZOEBOY

Bonswa Ms. Johnson.

RACHEL

Bon soir ZoeBoy.

ZOEBOY

Can I help you with anything?

RACHEL

If you could put those chips in that bowl, that'd be great.

ZoeBoy opens the bag. Starts filling the empty bowl.

RACHEL (CONT'D)

How's Fabiola?

ZOEBOY

She was running a slight temperature when I left but the doctor said she and the baby should both be okay.

Rachel finishes frosting the cake. Starts placing the candles

RACHEL

The hospital's not too far from school. I'll stop by tomorrow during my lunch period and check on her.

ZOEBOY

Thanks Ms. Johnson. I don't normally eat cake but that looks pretty good.

He pulls out a lighter. Hands it to Rachel.

ZOEBOY (CONT'D)

I hope Fab is as good a mom to our boy as you are to Dre.

RACHEL

Thanks baby, that's very sweet of you to say. But why you don't eat cake? Does diabetes run in your family?

ZOEBOY

No, it's just in Haiti we sometimes associate sugar with slavery.

Rachel starts lighting the candles.

ZOEBOY (CONT'D)

And it leaves a bad taste in my mouth.

INT. HOUSE - DINING ROOM - NIGHT - MOMENTS LATER

Rachel walks the sparkling confection to the dining room table as partygoers break out into the Stevie Wonder version of "Happy Birthday". She sets it down. Joins in the final chorus.

RACHEL & GUESTS

.... happy birthday to you!

Dre blows out the candles. A round of requisite applause is heard. His mom gives him a hug and a kiss.

RACHEL

Happy birthday baby. May the Lord's hand be upon all that you do this year and may your hands finally be upon some type of degree.

They both share a chuckle.

DRE

Thanks ma but you really need to stop riding me. I just read an article that said Americans are averaging 6 years to finish college.

RACHEL

Andre, you're a black man in America. You don't have the luxury of being average.

We hear a few "Preach mama", "Facts" and "True dats" from the crowd. Rachel starts cutting the cake. Dre's phone rings. He steps away.

INT. ESCALADE - MIAMI GARDENS - STREET - NIGHT

A pink Escalade is stopped at a red light. Behind the wheel sits SPELLS (20s, petite, Latina), rapping along to Cardi B. Nursing student by day, stripper by night. Drino rides shotgun, holding his burner to his ear. Can't hear Dre on the other line. Turns to Spells.

DRINO

I know it's all about pussy power and stripper solidarity but you think you could turn that shit down? I can't hear my boy.

INT. HOUSE - DINING ROOM - NIGHT - MOMENTS LATER

Dre hangs up. Walks back over. Rachel prepares a few more plates and hands them to ZoeBoy, who helps serve guests.

DRE

Hey ma, Drino's about to be here so we're gonna step out for a little bit. You need me to do anything before I go?

RACHEL

No, I'm good, thanks baby. He is coming in though, right? We need to get our group picture.

DRE

I don't think so. He sprained his ankle playing ball this afternoon and said he doesn't want to put any extra pressure on it.

RACHEL Okay, we'll just take it outside.

ZoeBoy finishes serving. Grabs a plate for himself.

RACHEL (CONT'D)

And Andre, I can tell you've been drinking so get a Lyft or let ZoeBoy drive tonight.

ZOEBOY That's right Andre.

He samples the cake. Pretty good.

ZOEBOY (CONT'D) Mama knows best.

EXT. HOUSE - STREET - MIAMI GARDENS - NIGHT - MOMENTS LATER

Rachel, Dre & ZoeBoy walk out of the house and up to the Escalade. Drino gets out gingerly, his foot in a soft WALKING BOOT. Spells stays inside, still bumping her music.

RACHEL

Damn Drino, your game is so trash you broke your own ankle?

She mimics a crossover then pretends to trip over her feet. Everybody shares a chuckle.

RACHEL (CONT'D)

I'm not gonna have to go down to the park like I did when you two were in middle school, am I?

DRINO

Nah, that's okay we're good.

DRE

Those 8th graders swore they had us beat til Ma went Lisa Leslie on that ass.

They smile, sharing a sweetly recalled memory. One of many.

DRINO

Them fools went home barefoot and broke.

Everybody laughs, enjoying the reminiscence. In the midst of her mirth, Rachel starts coughing a little. Dre notices.

DRE

You alright?

RACHEL

Yeah, I'm fine baby. Just my allergies acting up.

She pulls out her phone. Knocks on the Escalade window. Spells lowers it.

RACHEL (CONT'D)

Would you mind giving that Cardi B a break and taking this picture please?

SPELLS

It's City Girls but whatever just be quick. I'm due on stage in 20 minutes.

DRINO

Yo, you need to check that and watch the way you talk to Mama Johnson.

Spells hops out, slight attitude. Walks around the front of the truck. Rachel hands her the phone.

RACHEL

Thanks. It's a birthday tradition.

The group gathers next to Drino. Pose for the camera. FLASH!

INT. CAR - STREETS - NIGHT - LITTLE LATER

Reflected Supernova LED headlights flood ZoeBoy's windshield as a new white Ford F-150 blows past flying the Stars & Stripes. Drino rides shotgun in the blacked out Sentra. Dre sits in the back, hitting the Crown.

ZOEBOY

These American drivers think they own the road!

He lays on the horn. Curses in creole.

ZOEBOY (CONT'D)

Fout myed bouzin Americaine! (Fuck you American bitch!)

The light turns green. ZoeBoy takes off. Drino's burner phone rings. He pulls it out. Answers.

INT. PENTHOUSE - MIAMI BEACH - NIGHT - SAME TIME

A tall, striking man, VERNON WAINSCOTT, sits at a curved glass desk overlooking the ocean from his lushly appointed suite. Tumbler of top shelf Scotch in front of him. Phone to his ear.

VERNON

The word is you've lost a step and the veteran might soon be getting replaced by the rookie.

DRINO (O.S.)

You need a better source because that's nothing but fake news. I'm the black Cuban Lebron. Still at the top of my game and clutch when it counts.

VERNON

Good to hear. I would hate to think you were losing your edge.

He reaches into a humidor. Pulls out a finely aged Cuban.

DRINO (O.S.)

So to what do I owe the pleasure? I know you didn't call to talk about basketball.

VERNON

Let's just say a recent misfortune has befallen a few former associates and a new market opportunity now exists in your city.

In the background, we hear faint SCREAMS of anguish coming from the hidden chamber behind his bookcase.

VERNON (CONT'D)

I thought with the Road Runnas' ambition, you might want to fill the void. Nature abhors a vacuum and so do I.

He snips the cigar. The cries suddenly cease.

DRINO (O.S)

Hmm.. you know what I abhor? Taking on unnecessary risk in a highly competitive market. Nothing fails like success.

VERNON

Fair enough. High risk betas are like donkey dicks. Everybody's got one until it's time to drop trou and seal the deal. But remember this. Opportunity only dances for those on the dance floor.

DRINO (O.S.)

And what if we said yes?

VERNON

I'd have 25 pillows for your new store next week. 15 a pop. All feathers, no cotton.

DRINO (O.S.) I'll be in touch.

INT. CAR - STREETS - NIGHT

Drino hangs up. Breaks his burner in two. Looks to his boys.

DRINO

That was Vern.

DRE

The OG? What's he talking about?

DRINO

Some new turf just opened up. Thinks we should consider expanding across the city.

Dre reaches up front to get the Crown.

DRE

What's in it for him?

DRINO

Said he could start us with 25 pillows at 15 a pop. All feathers, no cotton.

ZOEBOY

That's a lot of weight to move.

DRE

Which would mean making new alliances or encroaching on rival turf. After the hit we took at L¥nk$'s today, might not our best move.

DRINO

I say we marinate on it. If we could make that math work a few times, we could probably exit ahead of schedule. Let's see how this kid Lalo's living.

ZoeBoy pulls up across from PTs, a local strip club. Parks.

DRINO (CONT'D)

Might be a way for him to start earning his Road Runna wings.

INT. PTS CLUB - NIGHT - MOMENTS LATER

The space is filled to capacity as sexy STRIPPERS of every stripe work their charms in the CROWD and on STAGE. Dre, ZoeBoy & Drino step inside.

DRE

I gotta uncage the mamba. I'll meet you upstairs.

He walks off. Drino scans the crowd. They start making their way through the club.

DRINO

You see your boy? What time you tell him to meet us?

ZOEBOY

I said to be here at 11.

He pulls out his phone. Checks it.

ZOEBOY (CONT'D)

Make a wish.

DRINO

For what, it ain't my birthday.

They keep moving. ZoeBoy shows him the time. 11:11.

ZOEBOY

Fab told me elevens are angel numbers so it's a good time to make a wish.

DRINO

I don't believe in angels.

ZOEBOY

Doesn't matter.

DRINO

Okay, I wish I was sitting on $100 mil, Megan Thee was my girl, and Halle Berry was my cougar.

ZOEBOY

That's three. You only get one.

They finally reach the bar. Six deep from every angle.

ZOEBOY (CONT'D)

And you're supposed to keep it to yourself.

INT. PTS CLUB - BATHROOM - NIGHT - SAME TIME

Lalo stands at a urinal, scrolling through his Instagram. A few other CLUB GOERS relieve themselves nearby. Dre walks in. Goes to the free stall. Lalo looks up from his phone. Checks Dre out.

DRE

You got a problem? Cause I ain't on no Lil Nas X shit...

(finishes, flushes)

... and staring at me like that will get you touched up.

LALO

Nah, my bad bro.

He puts his phone away. His swelling down considerably. Dre goes over to the sinks. Starts washing his hands.

LALO (CONT'D)

But you are Andre Johnson, right? Ain't that the dude's name in "black-ish"?

DRE

I don't know, I didn't watch that show. And who are you?

Lalo flushes. Zips up. Walks over. Dre sizes him up.

LALO

It's me, Lalo. ZoeBoy's people.

He starts rinsing his hands. Dre takes a close look.

DRE Oh shit, I ain't recognize you without the dreads.

Lalo finishes. Starts drying his hands.

LALO

Your boys here yet? I been here since 10:30 and ain't seen nobody.

DRE

Come on, I'm about to go meet them upstairs.

INT. PTS CLUB - VIP SECTION - MOMENTS LATER

The club's exclusive VIP area sits on the 2nd floor, overlooking the BAR, CROWD, & STAGE below. A GLASS WINDOW encircles the room, framing the space above the tables & booths.

Dre and Lalo enter. See Drino and ZoeBoy seated across the room. A cute table girl, KANDI (20s) takes their drink order as barely clad DANCERS/ESCORTS whisper in ears & vend their wares nearby.

KANDI

So that's two Crown rocks.

Drino nods. Dre and Lalo walk over. She turns to Dre.

KANDI (CONT'D)

And what's the birthday boy drinking tonight?

DRE

Apple Crown neat.

LALO

And I'll have a Mojito with Plantation 3.

She enters the order into her tablet then walks away.

DRINO

How you gonna order some disrespectful shit called Plantation with a table full of black people? You racist? One of them red hat wearing, blanco Latinos who think they better than everybody else?

LALO

Who, me? Nah, definitely not no racist. In fact, I'm almost black. I got 18% African on Ancestry.

Drino sizes him up. Face devoid of emotion. Then a slight grin.

DRINO

I'm just fucking with your 18% African ass.

Finishes his drink. Sets it down on the table.

DRINO (CONT'D)

That's why the world's so fucked up now. All these safe space snowflakes in their feelings over dumb shit.

Lalo breathes a sigh of relief. He and Dre take a seat.

ZOEBOY

I see you met Dre already and, of course, this is Drino.

LALO

Thanks for taking the meeting.

DRINO

We're only listening because ZoeBoy said you had heart. But it's Dre's birthday and I'm off my ADHD meds so you need to make it quick.

Lalo takes a moment to collect himself then jumps in.

LALO

Okay, so like I was telling ZoeBoy, I heard the Runnas might be looking to expand. (MORE)

LALO (CONT'D)

And if you do, with growth comes an increased need for quality laundry services. With my line of business...

DRINO

Which is what exactly?

LALO

I'm mostly an on-line broker of goods & services but I have a brick & mortar retail presence as well.

ZOEBOY

You should see his crib. Looks like Best Buy at Christmas.

DRE

So you run credit card scams and then re-sell the merch. How's that gonna help us?

LALO

Not only can I provide janitorial services for your cash, I could also supply new distribution channels for your product.

DRINO

We already got a maid. Besides, how do we know we can trust you? Just because somebody's got heart doesn't mean I can trust him.

ZOEBOY

No, but a soldier with heart is always an asset.

DRINO

Only if he's loyal and can be trusted.

DRE

So let's put his ass to the test. Trial by fire.

Kandi comes back with the order. Starts serving.

ZOEBOY

What about maintenance?

Dre takes his drink. Hits it. Considers.

DRE

Maintenance could work.

LALO

What the hell is maintenance?

DRINO

Let me think about it.

(stands up) I gotta piss.

INT. PTS CLUB - NIGHT - MOMENTS LATER

Drino heads for the stairs. As he nears the landing, three more VIPS are on the way up. One of them is small time albino hustler, YADIEL MONTOYA (Cuban, 30s aka Blanco). He's joined by two of his BOYS.

BLANCO

Look at this gimpy muthafucka. I thought Road Runnas was supposed to be fast. This puto can't even walk.

His friends laugh. Drino says nothing. Keeps moving.

BLANCO (CONT'D)

Not popping so slick now without your African bodyguard, huh?

Drino stops. Turns around.

DRINO

First of all, he's a Zoe and my brother, not my bodyguard. Now I told you once, send me your cleaning bill.

At the table, Lalo notices Drino stopped at the top of the stairs.

DRINO (CONT'D)

I'm not gonna keep repeating myself.

As Drino turns to go downstairs, Blanco winds up to SUCKER PUNCH him in the back of the head. Then, out of nowhere, CRACK! Lalo knocks Blanco OUT COLD with a beer bottle.

An all out BRAWL ensues. Dre, Lalo & ZoeBoy make quick work of Blanco's two boys. A yoked BOUNCER (30s) comes upstairs. Surveys the damage.

BOUNCER

Time to go fellas.

Drino hands him some cash. The bouncer pockets it.

BOUNCER (CONT'D)

Party time's over.

EXT. PTS CLUB - STREET - NIGHT - MOMENTS LATER

The four of them make their way outside. Still amped from the affray.

ZOEBOY

I told you the bull had heart! He knocked that coconut colored muthafucka out cold!

DRINO

No doubt. Good looks Lalo.

Drino turns, daps Lalo up, who beams in the adulation.

LALO

I had to do something Drino. Couldn't let him sneak you like that. Shit would've been disrespectful.

Drino grins at Lalo's levity.

DRE

So what's good? It's still early.

LALO

Sorry bro but I need to bounce. Gotta go check on my little brothers & sisters. He looks to ZoeBoy.

LALO (CONT'D)

You'll hit me up?

ZOEBOY

Cuando yo sepa algo, sabrás algo. (When I know something, you'll know something.)

INT. CAR - STREET - NIGHT - MOMENTS LATER

Dre, Drino & ZoeBoy cross the street. Get in the Sentra. ZoeBoy starts the engine. Puts on some Haitian music. Drino takes shotgun. Dre's in the back.

ZOEBOY

So, what do you think?

DRINO

About what, this weak ass dancehall, your boy, or where to next?

ZOEBOY

My boy. I gotta work early tomorrow so I'm taking you two back to Dre's.

DRE

Damn Haitian, sounds like impending fatherhood's making you soft.

DRINO

I don't know Books... think I'm ready to call it too. This foot's aching like a bitch.

DRE

I need to get both you geriatrics some Ensure. It's all good though, that honey Naz told me to hit her up after we're finished.

He pulls out his phone. Types a quick message.

DRINO

Good for you B, getting some birthday rizz. You earned that one. What's it been, 3-4 weeks?

ZOEBOY

Weeks?! Fabiola made me wait 6 months!

DRINO

6 months?! Shit, no wonder you married her.

DRE

You got played Haitian. Most American girls are fucking on the first night. Church girls on the second. Third if they're saved.

ZOEBOY

And Trump said I'm from the shithole country.
(changes the music) But for real, though. What do you think?

DRINO

I think sometimes he might overcompensate. A lot of pretty boys do.

DRE

Little napoleonic ones too.

DRINO

But I like his edge and if held in check, he could probably be useful.

(MORE)

DRINO (CONT'D)

My abuela outlived four husbands and always used to tell me. "Tame a wild beast and it'll be loyal for life."

ZOEBOY

So what should I tell him?

DRINO

Don't tell him anything. Let's see how he does with maintenance.

ZoeBoy pulls up in front of Dre's house. Parks.

DRINO (CONT'D)

And then we decide.

EXT. STREET - MIAMI GARDENS - NIGHT

Drino and Dre get out. ZoeBoy drives off. Dre pulls out his keys.

DRE

I'd drive you home bro but heavy is the head that drinks the Crown.

DRINO

It's all good B. I'm coming in while I wait for this Lyft, though.

(pulls out his phone)

I don't really mess with guacamole like that but I heard those wings were fire.

INT. HOUSE - MIAMI GARDENS - FRONT ROOM - NIGHT

Dre opens up the front door. Notices all of the lights are still on.

DRE

Ma? I hope you're not still up cleaning. I told you I'd do it the morning.

He heads towards the kitchen. Drino follows.

INT. HOUSE - KITCHEN - NIGHT - MOMENTS LATER

They walk in. On the floor in front of them, <u>Rachel lies unconscious.</u>

DRE

Mom?

He races over. Kneels down. Starts shaking her. No response. Turns to Drino.

DRE (CONT'D)

Call 911!

Drino pulls out his phone. Dials out.

INT. VAN - LITTLE HAVANA - NIGHT - SAME TIME

Lalo drives through his neighborhood listening to Miami rapper Bobby Biscayne. His phone RINGS. He answers. The line goes dead. He pulls up in front of his apartment building. Parks. Phone RINGS again. Different number. Doesn't answer this time.

EXT. STREET - LITTLE HAVANA - NIGHT - MOMENTS LATER

He gets out of the van. Starts walking to his building. Out of the shadows steps Blanco. Smoking a cigarette. Closes a flip phone.

BLANCO

¿No pensaste que me verías tan pronto, no maricón? (Didn't think you'd see me again so

soon did you bitch?)

Blanco FLICKS the cigarette in Lalo's eye. His boys quickly descend like spotted hyenas to a kill. As they ruthlessly stomp Lalo out, we...

INT. MIAMI JACKSON HOSPITAL - NIGHT - LATER

Dre & Drino sit outside a NURSE'S STATION in the Critical Care Unit. Drino's on the phone FaceTiming with his daughter ARIANNA (8).

DRINO

Why are you still up and not in bed like your brother? It's 3:30 in the morning! Where the hell's the sitter?!

ARIANNA

On the couch on Instagram live.

DRINO

Put her irresponsible ass on the phone!

We see the BABY SITTER (17, pretty), finishing her video in the background. Arianna walks over, hands her the phone.

ARIANNA

I don't think Daddy's too happy. He said a lot of bad words.

BABY SITTER

Hello?

As Drino steps away, a NURSE (40s, Latina) comes out of the station. Dre notices. Walks over.

DRE

Excuse me? Would you happen to have any information about my mom? She's in this unit.

The nurse looks up from her iPad. Gives Dre a once-over. Can tell he's been out partying.

NURSE 2

What's her name?

DRE

Rachel Johnson.

She types a few things into her ipad. Slight attitude.

NURSE 2

She's been admitted.

DRE

Is there any way I could see her?

NURSE 2

Not until the morning. Visiting hours start at 8. There are some couches in the lounge & the gift shop opens at 7 in case you want to freshen up.

She takes her iPad and returns to the unit. Drino finishes up with the baby sitter. Clicks off. Walks back over.

DRINO

What'd the nurse say?

DRE

She's been admitted. Said I could see her in the morning, so I think I'm just gonna crash in the lounge.

DRINO

Alright then Books, I'm gonna roll. Arianna's up Instagramming with the baby sitter and she's got boxing at 9.

He reaches out. They dap each other up.

DRINO (CONT'D)

Let me know what's good after you talk with the doctor.

INT. APARTMENT - LITTLE HAVANA - NIGHT - LITTLE LATER

Lalo sits at his kitchen table, nursing his wounds. One ICE PACK rests atop his right hand, another over his left BLACK EYE.

The apartment is modest but clean & nicely furnished. An assortment of consumer electronics BOXES crowd the space.

A door to one of the bedrooms opens. His little brother, SAMMY (10, on the Autism spectrum) comes out. Holds a WWE action figure in his hand. Walks over to Lalo, rubbing his eyes.

SAMMY

Lo siento Lalo. Traté de sostenerlo. (I'm sorry Lalo. I tried to hold it.)

We see a large WET SPOT in the front of his pajamas.

LALO

Está bien, no te preocupes. (It's okay, don't worry about it.)

He puts the ice packs down. Gets up from the table. Starts walking Sammy to the bathroom. Sammy motions to his black eye.

SAMMY

Qué pasó con tu ojo? (What happened to your eye?)

LALO

Me peleé de frente a un matón. (I got into a fight with a bully.)

SAMMY

Ganaste? (Did you win?)

LALO

Si, claro... Por qué? (Yes, of course... Why?)

They reach the bathroom door.

LALO (CONT'D)

No parece que gané? (Doesn't it look like I won?)

The brothers share a smile. Lalo opens the door and we ...

INT. MIAMI JACKSON HOSPITAL - ROOM - MORNING

Rachel sits up in bed, fully conscious and attentively listening to her doctor, DR. SATYA SINGH (30s, attractive.) A half eaten breakfast sits on a meal stand at her bedside.

Dre appears in the doorway holding a small plastic bag. Rachel looks up and smiles. Dr. Singh stops & turns.

DR. SINGH

You must be Andre. Your mom said you'd be here. I'm Dr. Singh, your mother's attending physician.

Dre walks over. Clearly hungover but looks a lot better. Gives his mom a kiss on the cheek then reaches into his bag and hands her a little stuffed bear. We'll recognize it as the same one from the opening scene.

DRE

The gift shop's not great but I thought you might like some company.

RACHEL

Thanks baby.

She puts it beside her in the bed. Smiles.

RACHEL (CONT'D)

It's perfect.

DRE

How you feeling?

An awkward silence hangs in the room. Dr. Singh intercedes.

DR. SINGH

Andre, your mother & I were just talking about some treatment options for her.

DRE

Treatment? For what?

She pauses a moment, hating to be the bearer of bad news.

DR. SINGH

Unfortunately, your mother's dealing with a fairly aggressive form of breast cancer. But we've detected it early & she's eligible for a new clinical trial that looks really promising.

Dre displays no emotion, wanting to remain strong for his mom.

DRE

Okay, so when can she start?

Rachel & Dr. Singh share a look. Dre notices.

DR. SINGH

The problem is your mother's primary insurance has lapsed so this new treatment wouldn't be covered.

DRE

How much are we talking about?

DR. SINGH

The trial lasts for six months at a cost of about $20,000 a month. $16,000 for the treatment and $4,000 for the medicine.

DRE

Dr. Singh, my mom's a teacher & I'm a college student. Besides breaking bad, is there anything else we could do?

Dr. Singh considers. Her compassion evident.

DR. SINGH

If you could come up with around half, say $60,000, we'll start the trial. Then you can make a payment plan for the rest. Otherwise we'll have to explore other options.

She waits for a beat, then gathers her things.

DR. SINGH (CONT'D)

I have other rounds to make this morning so why don't you discuss it with your mom and we'll talk later.

Dr. Singh leaves the room. Rachel turns to Dre.

RACHEL

Andre you know we don't have that kind of money.

DRE

No, but dad does. And if he can buy me the Vic and a new S-Class, he can pay for this.

RACHEL

Do not call your father for this money.

DRE

Why not? You'd rather die than accept his money? Didn't you always teach me that pride goes before the fall?

RACHEL

Andre, it's not pride. I just don't think he'd give it to you and I don't want you to be disappointed.

The nurse from last night comes in wheeling a cart.

NURSE 2

I'm sorry but I need to take your mom's vitals and then she needs to rest. Doctor's orders.

Dre nods. The nurse walks over. Scans Rachel's wrist band. Checks the monitor.

RACHEL

Baby, if God wants me to have that trial, he'll make a way.

DRE

I don't know Mom. I used to believe in God but honestly, right now...

He grabs his bag of toiletries. Gives her a peck on the cheek.

DRE (CONT'D)

I'm not even sure He exists.

INT. BOXING GYM - LITTLE HAVANA - MORNING

Arianna works a HEAVY BAG while her chubby little brother, OSCAR (5, cute), attempts to jump rope nearby. Drino stands nearby checking out the baby sitter's Instagram videos. His phone RINGS.

DRINO

Okay, good work. Now go get something to drink.

He hands Arianna some money. They scurry off. He yells after them.

DRINO (CONT'D)

And no pea protein bars for your brother! They give him diarrhoea and I'm the one who has to deal with the fall out.

EXT. MIAMI JACKSON HOSPITAL - MORNING - SAME TIME

Dre exits the hospital. Starts walking to the parking structure.

DRE

What up Drino? You guys still at the gym?

DRINO (O.S.)

Yeah, just sent the kids to go rehydrate and protein load. You talked to the doctor yet?

DRE

Breast cancer. She's eligible for a new trial but it's 60 sticks to start and I only got about 20 right now.

DRINO (O.S.)

Damn B, you know most of mine is caught up in our investments and crypto but I could come up with another 15 - 20.

DRE

I appreciate that bull but still leaves us 25 light.

INT. BOXING GYM - LITTLE HAVANA - MOMENTS LATER

Drino watches his kids at the vending machine, intimately aware of the damage a lost parent can do.

DRINO

You know what, fuck it. Tell the doctor it's covered.

DRE (O.S.)

What are you talking about?

DRINO

We'll pull the maintenance job, see what fruit that bears and then go from there.

DRE (O.S.)

But what about Lalo and the other two?

DRINO

I'll handle it.

DRE

Thanks brother.

DRINO

Always. Blood makes you relatives but loyalty makes you family.

Arianna and Oscar return. Immediately get back to work.

DRINO (CONT'D)

I'll hit ZoeBoy up after I'm done with the kids. Then we'll meet at the spot to start plotting.

INT. CAR - STREETS - LITTLE HAITI - EVENING

ZoeBoy drives through little Haiti listening to some reggaeton. Seated next to him, BLINDFOLDED, is Lalo.

ZOEBOY

Créeme hermano, es mejor así. Para tu propia protección. (Believe me brother, it's better this

way. For your own protection.)

He turns down an alley. Pulls up to an abandoned WARE-HOUSE. A large, ROLLED STEEL door stands before them.

ZOEBOY (CONT'D)

Si no te conviertes en Road Runner... (If you don't become a Road Runner...)

Dials a code on his phone. The smooth metal sheet slides open.

ZOEBOY (CONT'D)

... no deberías conocer nuestros secretos.

(...you shouldn't know our secrets.)

INT. WAREHOUSE - LITTLE HAITI - EVENING - MOMENTS LATER

ZoeBoy drives inside. Parks next to Dre's Crown Vic, still in the early stages of its restoration. Gets out. Walks around, open's his passenger's side door.

ZOEBOY

Vamos. (Let's go).

He grabs Lalo by the elbow. Leads him past an array of parked specialty vehicles - a COP CAR, MAINTENANCE VAN, EMT VAN, & another TAXI. The space is very clean and extremely well kept.

At a table in the back of the room, a few topless WOMEN bag up DRUGS under Dre's watchful eye. They all wear hair caps, latex gloves, bikini bottoms & ear plugs.

DRE

You think you're ready for this double R life Lalo? Shit's not all money, clubs & bitches you know.

ZoeBoy leads Lalo over to the maintenance van. Slides the door open. Inside, Drino sits behind the wheel in blue coveralls, no longer wearing his walking boot.

ZoeBoy helps Lalo get in, then climbs in himself. On the wall, we see an assortment of TACTICAL GEAR, UNIFORMS & accessories. Drino looks into his rearview mirror.

DRINO

Lalo, didn't think you'd make it.

He starts the engine. ZoeBoy removes Lalo's blindfold. His eye still black & swollen. Dre hops in. Slams the door shut.

DRINO (CONT'D)

Heard you had a pretty rough night.

INT. MAINTENANCE VAN - STREET - EVENING - MOMENTS LATER

The van pulls out into the street. Dre & ZoeBoy stash their phones in a hidden compartment, then start changing into navy coveralls like Drino's.

They add fake HAIR PIECES & WORK HELMETS with tinted VISORS.

Dre adjusts his wig. Gives Lalo the once over with slight disdain.

DRE

What size are you, a Small?

Lalo puffs his chest out a bit, stung by Dre's impertinence.

LALO

Medium.

Dre tosses him a pair of Large coveralls.

DRE

That's the smallest we got.

Lalo catches. Commences his wardrobe revision.

LALO

So what's the job?

DRINO

Should be a pretty quick lick. If the bird flies right, we'll net three bitches and a four point play.

Lalo looks confused. Dre translates for him.

DRE

The job should be pretty much in and out. If our intel is right, we should cop three keys of snow white and about $30 Gs.

LALO

And the venue?

DRINO

An apartment building on the 4th floor. 2 deep. No poppers.

LALO

That means cameras. You using silencers?

DRE

No, paint.

He reaches into the hidden compartment. Pulls out a .380. Puts it in his tool kit. ZoeBoy then helps himself to a Beretta 92. Attaches a silencer. Looks at Lalo.

ZOEBOY

You're good with this, right?

Lalo completes his change. Nods. ZoeBoy hands him a .22.

ZOEBOY (CONT'D)

Tal vez obtendrás una gran pistola después de ganar algo de peso. (Maybe you'll get a big boy

gun after you get your weight up.)

INT. MAINTENANCE VAN - STREET - NIGHT - LITTLE LATER

Drino pulls up in back of the Santa Rosa apartments in Allapattah, a 10 minute ride from Little Haiti. Parks.

DRINO

ZoeBoy, once we're in, you & Dre lock it down in the back then shut off the power. Me & Lalo will handle the emergency exits.

EXT. APARTMENT BUILDING - STREET - NIGHT - MOMENTS LATER

The four disembark from the van. Head for the rear of the building. At the back door, Drino pulls out a KEY. Opens it up. They all slip inside.

INT. APARTMENT BUILDING - ALLAPATTAH - NIGHT

As Drino & Lalo go to deal with the emergency exits, we stay with Dre & ZoeBoy. After securing the rear door with their NAIL GUNS, they make their way to the building's main PANEL BOARD, enclosed inside a chain-link cage.

ZoeBoy points to a CAMERA mounted down the hall. Dre nods, pulls his spray paint out of his tool kit and we...

INT. APARTMENT BUILDING - OFFICE - NIGHT - SAME TIME

The building's SECURITY GUARD (30's, dad bod) sits at his post watching porn on his phone. On the desk in front of him, we see two SURVEILLANCE MONITORS with feeds from throughout the building.

After a few moments, we notice one of them go DARK but the guard is too engrossed to notice. As he looks up and sees the lost signal, the POWER GOES OUT.

INT. APARTMENT BUILDING - HALLWAY - NIGHT - MOMENTS LATER

Drino & Lalo wait against the wall outside of the apartment. The building's emergency lights are on. Dre & ZoeBoy walk up quietly. Drino nods to ZoeBoy. ZoeBoy flips up his mask. Knocks.

ZOEBOY

Soy el muchacho de mantenimiento. Hay una problema en el edificio esta noche y estoy analizando los sistemas.(It's the maintenance

man. There's a problem in the building tonight and I'm analyzing the systems.)

INT. APARTMENT BUILDING - APARTMENT - NIGHT

Sitting on a couch inside is YAYO (25, Nicaraguan, thin). He gets up. Puts his phone in his pocket. Motions for his younger cousin, BETO (23, wiry), to put away all illicit items.

YAYO

Ya me voy.

He walks over to the door. Looks through the peep hole. Only sees ZoeBoy. We see his distorted image through the lens.

ZOEBOY

Tengo que verificar todos los apartamentos.(I have to check all of the apartments.)

Yayo checks with Beto then opens the door. ZoeBoy steps in. Notices Beto in the chair by the window. Formulates his plan.

ZOEBOY (CONT'D)

Gracias. No deberia tomar mucho tiempo.

(Thanks. It shouldn't take long.)

As he puts his toolbox down, ZoeBoy pretends to accidentally SHINE

THE FLASHLIGHT in Yayo's eyes, temporarily BLINDING him. Then he SWINGS the butt of his flashlight across Yayo's jaw, FRACTURING his mandible & dropping him UNCON-SCIOUS in place.

Beto pulls his piece and STARTS SPRAYING. ZoeBoy does a DIVE ROLL to avoid the barrage. A mounted 60" screen comes CRASHING to the ground. Shards of GLASS & DEBRIS shred the room.

Dre, Drino & Lalo come flooding into the apartment BLASTING back. Drino catches Beto twice in the chest, BLOWING him backwards & SMASHING against the window.

After the smoke clears, Drino & ZoeBoy go to check on Beto as Dre

& Lalo start tying up Yayo, binding his hands and feet with duct tape.

DRINO

You extract the bullets. We'll secure the bag.

ZoeBoy goes over to his tool kit. Pulls out a high powered MAGNET & some FORCEPS. Walks back over to the body.

Gets to work. Dre, Drino & Lalo start searching for the stash spot.

DRE

She said it was somewhere over by the window.

As ZoeBoy moves Beto's body to track the path of the bullets, a CRACK is exposed at the base of the window. Drino notices. Shines his lantern to examine the fissure more closely.

He pulls the window base towards him. It SLIDES OPEN. Inside, we see stacks of CASH & bricks of COKE. Drino makes a little noise. Dre goes to check it out. Impressed with the score.

DRINO

I think our little bird may have earned herself a bonus.

INT. APARTMENT BUILDING - NIGHT - MOMENTS LATER

The security guard stands in front of the building's main panel board, inspecting it with his flashlight. Notices it's been forced open.

Pulls his revolver. Starts walking back towards the front of the building when he sees four maintenance men coming down the back stairs. All wearing masks. He hurries after them.

SECURITY GUARD

Hey!

They turn back. See the guard advancing. TAKE OFF. Dre is first out the side door, followed by ZoeBoy then Drino, the surge of adrenaline serving as a panacea for his injured hoof.

Lalo struggles to keep up, his over-sized suit hindering his speed. As he finally runs out the side door, the left pocket of his coveralls GETS CAUGHT in the door handle and RIPS OFF, causing him to CRASH

TO THE GROUND.

The guard gives chase, revolver drawn. Tries to use the rear door to cut them off. SLAMS INTO IT. DOESN'T BUDGE.

SECURITY GUARD (CONT'D)

What the f--?!

Tries again. The rivets hold. Decides to use the EMERGENCY EXIT.

As he races out the door, his foot catches in a TRIPWIRE, causing him to trip & SHOOT HIMSELF below his chin, blowing out the TOP of his HEAD. Blood splattered grey matter litters the ground.

Lalo gets up off the ground, his clothes soiled with brain stains and blood. Limps past the body. Reaches the van. Gets inside. Slams the door shut, his life forever changed.

Drino fires up the engine and drives off as the faint din of sirens wail in the distance...

EXT. APARTMENT BUILDING - NIGHT - LITTLE LATER

McCluskey walks up on the crime scene in street clothes. A uniformed cop, HECTOR SANCHEZ, (30s, Puerto Rican) cordons off the area with yellow tape.

MCCLUSKEY

What do we got Sanchez?

Sanchez turns around, recognizing the voice.

SANCHEZ

Don't you have anything better to do on your night off, McCluskey?

MCCLUSKEY

Come on Sanchez, you know my old lady just left me. This gives me something to do besides getting drunk and stalking her online.

Sanchez considers, finally relents.

SANCHEZ

One deceased male. Hispanic. Building's security guard. Appears to be self inflicted.

McCluskey starts scanning the area.

MCCLUSKEY

Anything else?

SANCHEZ

Two more bodies on the 4th floor. One deceased male, early 20s. Other's a teenager. Jaw broken in two places. Poor kid will be lucky to talk again.

MCCLUSKEY

You wouldn't happen to know the apartment would you? Me & Esperanza have been investigating a Nicaraguan drug cartel that operates out of this building.

SANCHEZ

May have been 408, but don't quote me.

MCCLUSKEY

Thanks Sanchez. You're one of the good ones. I'm glad your family made it to America before Trump had a chance to complete his wall.

SANCHEZ

Fuck you McCluskey. My family was in south Florida when yours was still living in Ireland eating potatoes and fucking sheep.

McCluskey starts walking to his car. Pulls out his phone. Dials. The person on the other end answers but says nothing.

MCCLUSKEY

We've got a problem. The Santa Rosa just got hit.

He reaches his car. A black GMC SUV.

MCCLUSKEY (CONT'D)

... and there are bodies to account for.

INT. WAREHOUSE - LITTLE HAITI - NIGHT

Dre puts the last remaining stacks of CASH into a polished aluminum briefcase. Behind him, Drino supervises the girls while Lalo sits blindfolded in a chair nearby. He closes the case.

DRE

That's $33,000.

Hands it to ZoeBoy, now wearing a designer, European cut suit.

ZOEBOY

What about Lalo?

DRE

You just clorox the cash. We'll take care of your boy.

EXT. HIALEAH PARK RACING & CASINO - NIGHT - LITTLE LATER

ZoeBoy walks up to the Hialeah Park Casino entrance along a beautiful palm tree-lined path. In front of him, water majestically flows over a fountain, evoking the elegance of an Italian piazza.

INT. HIALEAH PARK RACING & CASINO - NIGHT - MOMENTS LATER

He goes inside. The main floor is packed with GAMBLERS playing slots, electronic Roulette & Black Jack. MUSIC pumps as cute COCKTAIL WAITRESSES scurry about filling drink orders.

He makes his way past the machines and heads towards a SWEEPING STAIRCASE that leads to the POKER ROOM upstairs on the 2nd floor.

INT. HIALEAH PARK RACING & CASINO - POKER ROOM - NIGHT

Two double GLASS DOORS open. ZoeBoy enters. Heads over to the CASHIER'S CAGE. An armed GUARD stands sentinel. Inside is Dre's friend, Naz.

NAZ

Good evening sir & welcome to Hialeah Park, south Florida's biggest poker room. How may I help you?

ZoeBoy hands her the case. She takes it, opens. Pulls out the bands of cash. Runs them through a counter like a bank teller. Then starts counting out CHIPS and placing them in a silver case.

NAZ (CONT'D)

There you go sir. Your $30,000.

She slides it over. We see a shot of his receipt. Four deposits of $7,500 each. Hands him a key for his safe deposit box.

NAZ (CONT'D)

Good luck.

INT. HIALEAH PARK RACING & CASINO - POKER ROOM

ZoeBoy walks to one of the tables in the back of the room. Seated there is McCluskey's partner, Esperanza. He puts his case down. Takes a seat.

ZOEBOY

Deal me in.

INT. CROWN VICTORIA - STREET - NIGHT - SAME TIME

Dre drives his Crown Vic through little Havana. Drino rides shotgun. Lalo sits in the back, still blindfolded. They pull up in front of Lalo's building.

DRINO

Say nothing to nobody.

He reaches into the back. Takes off Lalo's blindfold.

DRINO (CONT'D)

Or the guard won't be the only one meeting an untimely demise.

Lalo nods. Gets out. Closes the door. Dre pulls off.

DRE

Little neph showed some heart tonight.

DRINO

Yeah, but his ass got lucky. Without the tripwire, that slow muthafucka probably gets caught and then we'd all have a problem.

INT. HIALEAH PARK RACING & CASINO - POKER ROOM - NIGHT

ZoeBoy sits at the table examining his hand. His case of chips nearly depleted. On the table before him, we see the three card spread: 10 of Hearts, Ace of Diamonds, King of Spades.

He lifts his two cards. We see Ace of Spades, King of Diamonds. Lays them back down.

DEALER

The bet is to you sir.

ZoeBoy slides over a stack of chips. Esperanza regards her cards. Sees ZoeBoy's bet. We notice her collection of chips has grown appreciably. The dealer throws the turn. 8 of Clubs. Looks to Esperanza.

DEALER (CONT'D)

The bet is now yours.

She checks. ZoeBoy decides to go all in. Pulls his remaining chips. Puts them into the pot The dealer looks to Esperanza.

DEALER (CONT'D)

He's all in with his final $5,000.

Esperanza looks at her cards one last time. Sees his bet. The dealer throws the final card: Queen of Diamonds.

The dealer turns over his two cards. 8 of Hearts, Jack of Hearts. Then ZoeBoy: 2 pair. Ace-King. Finally, Esperanza: Queen of Spades, Queen of Clubs. 3 Queens wins. She pulls her winnings towards her.

ZoeBoy finishes his drink. Gets up from the table.

EXT. PTS CLUB - BACK LOT - NIGHT

The Crown Vic is parked in the back lot of PTs. Drino sits inside the car while Dre stands outside the club's back door. The door OPENS. We see Dre hand the table girl, Kandi, a KEY & BAND of CASH. They have a brief exchange. She goes back inside.

INT. CROWN VICTORIA - PTS CLUB - BACK LOT - MOMENTS LATER

Dre returns to the car. Gets in.

DRINO

I know she was happy to get that extra bread. Bitches love to eat.

DRE

Yeah, but not so happy about those two bodies.

DRINO

Nobody's happy about them but it's the cost of doing business. Now we got the funds for your mom and after we flip these pillows a few times, we can be out of the game for good.

They share a smirk, considering the possibilities. Drino's new burner phone PINGS. He opens it, reads a text from ZoeBoy: WE'RE DONE.

DRINO (CONT'D)

Looks like everything just made it through the spin cycle.

INT. GMC TRUCK - STREET - NIGHT

McCluskey sits in his truck. Sees Sanchez and his partner get into their squad car and drive off. Pulls out his phone. Makes a call.

MCCLUSKEY

They just left. You need to make it quick.

EXT. STREET - NIGHT - MOMENTS LATER

McCluskey gets out. Goes to the back of the truck. Opens the hatch. Grabs a roll of POLICE TAPE. A blacked out Cadillac DeVille pulls up behind him. Parks. Shuts it lights.

The DeVille's driver's side door opens. Out steps Vernon. Exchanges no pleasantries with McCluskey.

They start walking. Reach the back of the building. Pass through the yellow tape. Walk up to the rear door. Vernon pulls out a set of keys.

INT. APARTMENT BUILDING - NIGHT - MOMENTS LATER

They enter the building. Power still hasn't been restored. Head to the rear stairwell. Start walking up.

Exit on the 4th floor. Go to 408. McCluskey looks around. Takes a picture of the door. Then rips down the police tape. Vernon pulls his keys out. Opens the door.

INT. APARTMENT - NIGHT - MOMENTS LATER

They go inside. The apartment is as we last saw it. Bullet holes infest the walls. Beto's body remains bloodied on the floor. McCluskey shuts the door. As soon as it closes, Vernon SLAPS the shit out of him.

VERNON

Don't you ever tell me what to do! You might have a badge and the complexion for the protection, but I still own your ass. Never forget it.

A small trickle of blood drips from McCluskey's mouth. He wipes it, seething but composed. Vernon's phone vibrates. He pulls it out. Sees it's Drino. Answers.

INT. CROWN VICTORIA - STREET - NIGHT - SAME TIME

The Crown Vic is parked under an industrial bridge with its lights off. Drino holds the burner to his ear. Dre sits next to him.

DRINO

I talked to my chiropractor. Said I should invest in a few new pillows.

In front of them, another CAR pulls up. Because of its head-lights, we can't really tell the make or model. Parks. Shuts off its lights. Dre gets out.

INT. APARTMENT - NIGHT

Vernon surveys the carnage before him.

VERNON

You have three days or the terms change. It's a highly competitive market.

He stands over Beto's body. Looks in disgust as he shines his flashlight on the empty drug cache.

INT. CAR - STREET - NIGHT

Dre sits in the front passenger seat. Esperanza hands him an envelope.

VERNON (O.S.)

And I'm going to need you and your boys to help me find some people.

Dre looks inside. A check for $25,000. Esperanza's phone vibrates.

VERNON (O.S.) (CONT'D)

They've committed the cardinal sin of taking what's mine...

She checks her message. Turns to Dre.

ESPERANZA

We need to watch our back. I think McCluskey might be dirty.

VERNON (O.S.)

... and the wages of that sin is death.

The line goes dead. Drino flips his phone shut. Dre gets back in. Starts the car. They drive off exultantly into the foreboding south Florida night, unaware of the darkness they have just unleashed.

They will soon discover otherwise.

<u>END OF PILOT</u>

www.ingramcontent.com/pod-product-compliance
Lightning Source LLC
Chambersburg PA
CBHW071459130726
47997CB00006B/2397